AN ADVENT ANTIPHONS

Fr Jonathan Munn OblOSB

Published by the Anglican Catholic Church – Diocese of the United Kingdom

© 2019 Fr Jonathan Munn OblOSB. All rights reserved

ISBN 978-0-244-77253-6

Contents

Introduction 5

Benedictus 6

Magnificat 7

First Sunday in Advent 8

    Monday 11

    Tuesday 13

    Wednesday 15

    Thursday 17

    Friday 19

    Saturday 22

Second Sunday in Advent 24

    Monday 28

    Tuesday 31

    Wednesday 33

    Thursday 36

    Friday 40

    Saturday 43

Third Sunday in Advent 44

    Monday 47

    Tuesday 50

    Ember Wednesday 52

Thursday 54

Ember Friday 57

Ember Saturday 59

Fourth Sunday in Advent 61

Monday 62

Tuesday 63

Wednesday 64

Thursday 65

Friday 66

The Great Advent Antiphons on the Magnificat 67

December 16th 67

December 17th 68

December 18th 70

December 19th 71

December 20th 72

December 21st 74

December 22nd 75

December 23rd 76

Vigil of the Nativity 77

Feast of the Nativity 78

Introduction

Many Benedictine Oblates use the Monastic Diurnal to pray their Daily Offices. In Advent, each day has particular antiphons written for it at Lauds and Vespers. Each antiphon is a short verse, or an allusion to a verse from the Gospel reading for the Sunday that begins each week. Since these antiphons are peculiar to each day of Advent, a short Reflection on what they mean for us is worthwhile and allows us to enter into the practice of devoting one's time each day during this season of fast, penitence and prayer. This little collection of Reflections arises from *Lectio Divina* on these antiphons and it is hoped that they will allow the reader to find some assistance in the practice of devotion during Advent. We also include the collects and the texts of the Benedictus and Magnificat so that, if any wish to incorporate this work as part of their daily prayer through Advent, they may do so accordingly.

JMM+ Feast of St Athanasius 2017

Benedictus

Blessed be the Lord God of Israel :
for he hath visited and redeemed his people;
And hath raised up a mighty salvation for us :
in the house of his servant David;
As he spake by the mouth of his holy Prophets :
which have been since the world began;
That we should be saved from our enemies :
and from the hand of all that hate us.
To perform the mercy promised to our forefathers :
and to remember his holy Covenant;
To perform the oath which
he sware to our forefather Abraham :
that he would give us;
That we being delivered out of the hand of our enemies :
might serve him without fear;
In holiness and righteousness before him :
all the days of our life.
And thou, Child, shalt be called the Prophet of the Highest:
for thou shalt go before the face of the Lord
to prepare his ways;
To give knowledge of salvation unto his people :
for the remission of their sins,
Through the tender mercy of our God :
whereby the day-spring from on high hath visited us;
To give light to them that sit in darkness,
and in the shadow of death :
and to guide our feet into the way of peace.

Glory be to the Father, and to the Son :
and to the Holy Ghost;
As it was in the beginning, is now, and ever shall be :
world without end. Amen.

Magnificat

MY soul doth magnify the Lord :
and my spirit hath rejoiced in God my Saviour.
For he hath regarded : the lowliness of his hand-maiden.
For behold, from henceforth :
all generations shall call me blessed.
For he that is mighty hath magnified me :
and holy is his Name.
And his mercy is on them that fear him :
throughout all generations.
He hath shewed strength with his arm :
he hath scattered the proud in
the imagination of their hearts.
He hath put down the mighty from their seat :
and hath exalted the humble and meek.
He hath filled the hungry with good things :
and the rich he hath sent empty away.
He remembering his mercy hath holpen his servant Israel :
as he promised to our forefathers,
Abraham and his seed, for ever.

Glory be to the Father, and to the Son :
and to the Holy Ghost;
As it was in the beginning, is now, and ever shall be :
world without end. Amen.

First Sunday in Advent

Antiphon on Magnificat (First Vespers)

Behold, the Name of the Lord † cometh from afar: and His glory filleth all the earth.

Reflection

"Name" is a word that we can trivialise through over-familiarity, yet these little syllable speaks of things far beyond its utterance. To name something gives us power and knowledge of that thing. We can work out its rules, determine its nature, and understand its identity. The name of a thing tells us what that thing must be. Yet, as we stand here watching and waiting for the Nativity, we know that the Name of the Lord is coming. Surely this Name confounds our attempts to pin it down with the intellect? Did not God give a cryptic name from the burning bush? I AM! Yet, that name tells us that God not only exists, but existence is in His very nature, and that He causes all things to exist.

But the Name of the Lord is coming. This is a Name that humanity has only heard in old-time prophecies. This is a Name for which the oppressed have longed, for which those beaten down by sin – theirs and others – have turned their faces to the sky in hope, for which those caught in the snares of darkness have searched with the tiny light of truth hidden in the words of a previous generation likewise ensnared.

The Name of the Lord is coming and will do exactly what It says!

Collect

Stir up Thy might, we beseech Thee, O Lord, and come; that we who are ever threatened by the peril of our sins, may be counted worthy to be rescued by Thy protection, and saved by Thy deliverance. Who with God the Father, in the unity of the Holy Ghost, livest and reignest God, world without end. Amen.

Antiphon on Benedictus

The Holy Ghost † shall come upon thee, Mary; fear not, thou shalt bear in thy womb the Son of God, alleluia.

Reflection

Fear not? With a reputation to be shattered? With a husband-to-be to embarrassed and lost? With nine months of physical toil peculiar to the pregnant? With paltry means to care for another mouth, especially if that husband abandons her? Surely, there's lots to fear!

Yet Mary knows that if an Angel of God tells her not to fear, then all her concerns, whether they come to pass or not, will not be a part of her destiny. She may be daunted, but she knows that God is with her, more intimately than any other human being who has ever lived. There will be pain, anguish, and deep sadness. There will be difficulty, hardship, fingers pointed, whispers and glances.

The Son of God is coming, piercing souls by nailing them to Him on the Cross, and through the Cross enjoining them to God in Eternity. Eternity trumps pain, for pain begins and pain ends. There is nothing to fear, Eternity's sun is about to rise.

Antiphon on Magnificat (Second Vespers)

Fear not, Mary, † for thou hast found favour with the Lord: behold, thou shalt conceive, and bring forth a Son, alleluia.

Reflection

God's favour seems to come with a lifetime of difficulty, but perhaps that point of view comes with our tendency to focus on the negative aspects of life and see them as preventing life from being lived. God says, "No!" In living a life as the Mother of God with all that this name demands, Mary lives a real life. It is not an inauthentic life lived on the sidelines, waiting for the credits to roll before the next episode begins. In finding favour with God, Mary demonstrates to Him her desire to be alive, to participate in His life, to be a real human being, not a pale imitation wandering through Time before ceasing to be.

Getting stuck in to the business of living is messy. God gets His hands covered with the dust of the earth as He creates Man in His own image. His Son gets His hands covered with His own blood in order to bring humanity into the Light of Creation and the fullness of life therein. Likewise, those who are to live life must expect mess and pain, not as things to fear, but as things which signify our desire to be born, to live and to love the One who gives us life. Mary does this and becomes the Queen of Heaven.

Monday

Antiphon on Benedictus

The Angel of the Lord ☨ announced unto Mary, and she conceived by the Holy Ghost.

Reflection

Such familiar words recited morning, noon, and night. In praying the Angelus, we entwine our day with the Incarnation of Our Lord, cloaking it in the mystery of God made Man. From the moment that we recite it in the morning, the day becomes pregnant with God's will united with our intentions. As we recite it at noon, we unite the labours of the day with all its blood, sweat and tears, with the holy blood, sweat and tears shed by Our Lord upon the Cross, and with His Mother who suffers the sword piercing her own soul. In reciting it in the evening, we commit the service of our labour to God, as the Lord completes the work of Redemption with the triumphant cry of "It is finished!"

It is only with our Advent before the throne of Grace that the labours of our days find their true completion. We long to hear, "well done, thou good and faithful servant," and we shall, by seeking first the Kingdom of God in our lives, just as Our Lady sought Him whom she did not yet know, but would know more intimately than any other human being.

Antiphon on Magnificat

Lift up thine eyes, † O Jerusalem, and see the power of the King: behold, the Saviour cometh to loose thee from thy chain.

Reflection

Sin has a double edged sword. Not only does it separate us from God, it lies to us that we can never be reconciled with God. Habitual Sin wields this sword so keenly, preying not only upon our weaknesses and fallen nature with seductions and temptations, but gleefully stirring up the guilt when we fall for the thousandth time, convincing us that we have committed that sin for the 491st time and that we can no longer be forgiven. We grieve for our habitual sins, and yet commit them again. Why? Because we are focussed on the chain that binds us, to the exclusion of all else. It is a chain that we cannot break of ourselves, struggle though we do.

What should we do? Look up. Look away from the sin. Forget about it, by looking into the eyes of the One who comes to save. Look up and work in your life to prepare for His arrival. Look up and see that it is He alone who possesses the strength to wrest asunder the links which bind us to the earth and to Hell. Let not sin have the upper hand, by acknowledging that you are a sinner, but that you are also the precious Creation of God who not only seeks to save you from all your sins, but actually does so! Look up to see Him, and forget all else.

Tuesday

Antiphon on Benedictus

Before they came together † Mary was found with Child of the Holy Ghost, alleluia.

Reflection

How many marriages have been conducted with the bride holding a strategically placed bouquet to cover the fact that she is with child? Yet, these days, there is less shame for brides to be present at their wedding with their children playing a part. While we bewail the tendency of modern folk to put the cart before the horse, nonetheless, the presence of a bride and groom together with their children does solidify that family in the eyes of God. There is love here in this commitment which does need to be recognised perhaps even above how morally questionable it has been grown.

Yet, the love of a husband is perfected in the love of St Joseph for Our Lady. The child is not his, he knows it, his wife knows it and, if this is common knowledge among the Evangelists, it is known to a wider circle within the community. Some may point to the immoral actions of Our Lady and St Joseph, or to the oppressive demands of a Roman Soldier. Certainly, this world recognises him as the father of the child. Yet, as the womb encloses the life of the Holy Infant, so does the couple's love for each other enclose the sanctity of His conception.

Antiphon on Magnificat

Seek ye the Lord † while He may be found: call upon Him while He is near, alleluia.

Reflection

What a strange saying! When is the Lord far from us? Will He not make Himself known to any who seek Him?

No. For He tells His disciples, "Unto you it is given to know the mysteries of the kingdom of God: but to others in parables; that seeing they might not see, and hearing they might not understand."

There are those who will seek God as one would seek a genie or an oracle to do one's bidding or tell the future; there are those who seek God as the justification for their own way of living; there are those who seek God to put Him in the test-tube and measure His statistics. None of these will find Him even though they seek fastidiously and methodically: the do not know Whom they seek.

We seek first the kingdom of God and His Righteousness, together and not as separate entities. We seek Him as our ruler and our good. We seek Him in the fallenness and degradation of our own hearts weeping for our sins as we walk in our darkness and long for the light. We seek Him in our humility and are presented with no Imperial Person of Opulence and Power, but rather a tiny baby struggling to find rest in among the cattle feed. This is the God Who is near and desires our proximity. However, the paradox is that, while He is always ready to be found, we can be too far away to find Him.

Wednesday

Antiphon on Benedictus

Out of Sion † shall go forth the law, and the word of the Lord from Jerusalem.

Reflection

Surely, Our Lord is born in Bethlehem, not Jerusalem. It is outside Jerusalem that He dies cast out like a common criminal. How can this be the testimony of His birth?

It is the totality of the Incarnation that saves us. We do not say that it is from 14:59 and 59 seconds on Good Friday that we are saved. It is the whole Christ, Divine and Human who leads us out of darkness into light. It will be in Jerusalem that He will preach, first from the Old Testament and then from the New and then from the New Jerusalem coming down from Heaven. And He will preach the truth, the way things are, the way things God ordained.

This is not a law written down and ratified by judges and politicians, by scribes and Pharisees. This is a law, like that of gravity which we may only describe through arcane mathematics and theoretical physics. It is the state of reality itself and we learn of it through the word preached and from the criminal thrown out of the city and crucified upon the Tree.

Both Jew and Gentile can receive this Word and take it to heart because it comes from Jerusalem for the Jew and passes out into all the world for the Gentile. The language is not Hebrew, Greek, Latin nor English, but the language of love in which the Incarnation is written from its Conception and Nativity to the Crucifixion and Resurrection and beyond.

The coming of Christ is the coming of the law and the word. All may celebrate its arrival, if they wish.

Antiphon on Magnificat

After me † cometh one mightier than I, the latchet of whose shoes I am not worthy to unloose.

Reflection

What is this God Who will allow a woman to change His dirty nappies, will choose to suckle at her breast, who will need winding, washing and cuddles? What is this God Who suffers the intimate touch of human beings in complete helplessness and smallness? Why are we so worthy to be presented with this tiny baby to be born among us? It is truly a scandal that God in all His Majesty prefers the swaddling clothes and soiled clothes of infancy. But the scandal goes further.

The one whose feet we are unworthy to wash is the one who washes our feet in service. In so doing, He subverts all we know about worth, importance, majesty and power. In the act of being born, He prevents the whole "holier than thou" attitude that false piety tries to grow in the self-righteous soul. In powerlessness, He shows that our might, strength and majesty are piffle and folly. In poverty, He shows that our wealth and sense of worth are skewed and paltry. In taking our humanity, He shows that human beings are worth more than anything the universe can possess.

Thursday

Antiphon on Benedictus

Blessed art thou ☦ among women, and blessed is the fruit of thy womb.

Reflection

While the announcement of a pregnancy is for many people an occasion of great joy, the facts of pregnancy are hard work, unglamorous, and filled with worry. At every stage, the question hangs over us, "is the baby okay?" The baby lies hidden, covered by the mother's flesh. While, in the later month, the baby can be felt moving and wriggling, moments of quiet can raise those doubts.

Pregnancy is hard work, and many do not end happily but rather in the most profound sorrow and darkness for those who were expecting to become parents. Where is the blessedness of that womb?

It is doubtful that Our Lady was completely free from this worry, herself. Although she had an angelic annunciation and the promise of a baby, all around her in her community would have been the signs of pregnancies that did not go full term. She would have known women who died during labour.

Yet, she does see the death of her son, so horribly. How blessed is the fruit of her womb on the Cross?

It is the sorrows of Our Lady that she bears with us that give us hope. While she may have had a successful pregnancy, the Queen of Heaven knows great grief and thus is able to stand beside us as we mourn the deaths of those whose lives had so brief a span. If she stands with us, then Our Lord does not stand far away. Where there is the agony of the Cross, so there is the joy of new life even though that joy may seem so far away as to be a little glimmer on the horizon of despair. The blessedness of Our Lady and the blessedness of her son, Our Lord, show the dignity of ever having been alive. Where there is blessedness, there is life. Where there is life, there is hope.

<u>Antiphon on Magnificat</u>

I will wait † upon the Lord my Saviour: and I will look for him while he is near, alleluia.

Reflection

In everyone's prayer life, there are periods of activity and inactivity. There are times when we find ourselves in the Waiting Room, listening out for the call. There are times when we even feel that we're looking for the door to the Waiting Room in the first place.

What is it that we're waiting for? A call into a headmaster's office? A job interview? The results of a medical? It is how we perceive God to be for us that affects how we wait for Him and how we expect to wait upon Him. We have an idea of who we are and what our talents are, and what our needs are. However, we know that God knows us better than we know ourselves.

Might it be that the Waiting Room is for us to realise something about ourselves? Might it be that we're not actually alone in the Waiting Room and that it is God being near who awaits our realisation so that we can serve Him by being the person that He created.

Friday

Antiphon on Benedictus
Lo, there cometh one † that is both God and Man, of the house of David, to sit upon the throne, alleluia.

Reflection
Again, we find ourselves faced with the question as to how an ever-present God can have an Advent. As this Advent is to progress, we find the Cloud of Unknowing form around us as we experience that which is utterly unique which appears to contradict all that we know: the Word becomes flesh and dwells with us.

We see, in the baby in the manger, a condensation of the presence of God – a condensation that the world has not known since the days of Eden. This baby is a condensation through the line of human ancestry. Every baby has two parents, four grandparents, eight great-grandparents – a countless chain of doubling backwards in time and thus a halving forwards in time for it is with this baby that the line will terminate. Yet, in the baby that is to come, we can trace the line of David, a line of God's interaction with humanity documented within Holy Scripture. The line of David may terminate in the Christ Child, but this its finality transcends time, for here is the Omega of God reaching from His Alpha in Eden.

In thinking of the multiplicity of our ancestors, we must come to the revelation that we are all related somewhere along the line. We may not be related in a way that can be named succinctly such as "great-uncle" or "first cousin" but we come to realise that we are indeed all related as a common humanity: we are related to David and thus to Christ. This line of David stretches like a vine throughout Humanity's history connecting us all. And this is why its termination in the Head bids us love one another as we love ourselves.

Antiphon on Magnificat

Out of Egypt † have I called my Son: He shall come to save His people.

Reflection

Out of Egypt comes the people of God – first the Hebrews and then their Messiah and our Saviour and, as a consequence of this, we ourselves. It is important that we do not regard Egypt in a literal sense. We cannot regard all Egyptians as being our enslavers. This is the mistake that the Devil has persuaded men to seek to exterminate the Jews because "they crucified Our Lord". The grammatical concept here, which many miss, is that of synecdoche – the part standing for the whole.

The Jews are a synecdoche for humanity: WE crucify the Lord, each one of us when we fall to Sin, its bondage and its deadly consequence. Each of us who sin must bear that responsibility and not put the blame on a scapegoat. Egypt stands for our slavery to which we submit ourselves willingly when we choose to reject God. Our Lord is brought into Egypt by His parents in order to find sanctuary from the evil of man, just as we are brought into a sinful world by our parents. And out of Egypt He is borne, once more by His parents just as we will be carried out of our slavery of Sin with Him by Our Father in Heaven.

In clinging to Christ with the faith that He gives us, we receive the reality of salvation. We do not cling on to our own righteousness and thus try and make a scapegoat of others, hoping that their removal from the world will make Heaven happen on Earth. We acknowledge our sins and, in repentance, we are brought out of slavery to the land that God promises us if we hold fast to Him in faith.

Saturday

Antiphon on Benedictus
Fear not, † O Sion, behold thy God cometh, alleluia.

Reflection

Earthly Sion has seen many a tribulation. Times of prosperity have been met with times of degradation, despoiling and destruction. The temple at Jerusalem has come and gone and we may never see its like again – at least not as we would expect.

The Jerusalem that we do expect is coming down from God and is more beautiful than words can describe, though Holy Scripture sets the pattern. And God comes to this New Jerusalem as the Bridegroom to His Bride. We should not be frightened of the sexual imagery here, for it is in this end-time of consummation that the act of union between bride and groom is truly sanctified.

Human beings have made sex so sordid, and something to be ashamed of, forgetting its divine creation and its ordinance. We praise virginity because of its freedom from the lascivious lusts of fallen men and women, yet the loving couple, married in the hope of generating and extending their love to embrace their children are no less chaste and no less holy.

God saves by giving Himself in an act of sanctification through His own sacrifice. All that is human is perfected and purified in this act for God does not hate what He has made but wills its fulfilment in Himself. We look at our uncleanness and we fear what will become of our familiarity with our fallen selves. If we believe that God made us and submit to ourselves as His Creation, then His advent will mean an end to our sullied humanity and an eternal glory in sharing His divinity.

Second Sunday in Advent

Antiphon on Magnificat (First Vespers)

Come, O Lord in peace; † visit us with Thy salvation, that we may rejoice before Thee with a perfect heart.

Reflection

We bear the image of God: our joy is an image of His joy; our love is an image of His love; our peace is an image of His peace. Yet the presence of sin in the world means that these images are marred and distorted, but not obliterated for God Himself demonstrates that He can stand alongside Humanity in the feebleness of the Human frame. Perfection is something He offers us.

Our Lord was not born perfect. That is not to say that He sinned or bore the cracks in Human Nature caused by our sins. Rather, it demonstrates that Our Lord's life and work were not complete until the great, terrible and final cry of "*tetelestai*!" upon the Cross. Almost untranslatable into English and nonetheless translated, "it is finished!" it has the realisation of perfection that Christ's coming is complete.

We seek our perfection not only in the completion of our creation realised upon our death-beds and carried through to the Divine Judgment, but also in the healing of sin's wounds which make Death a wage earned. Our tenuous grasp of peace is perfected in the stable balance of Christ's peace. Our hearts are perfected when they are pierced by the lance of love just as Our Lord's loving heart was pierced by the lance of war. Our happiness ruled by chance, change and circumstance is perfected by God's joy. These can be glimpsed through the windows of our being into God's own self. We can extend that glimpse through prayer and actively loving our neighbour.

Collect

Stir up our hearts, O Lord, to make ready the ways of Thine Only-Begotten; that by his coming we may be worthy to serve Thee with purified minds. Through the same Jesus Christ, Thy Son, Our Lord, who liveth and reigneth with Thee in the unity of the Holy Ghost, God, world without end. Amen

Antiphon on Benedictus

Now when John had heard † in the prison the works of Christ, he sent two of his disciples, and said unto Him: Art Thou He that should come, or do we look for another?

Reflection

There are two types of doubt; one is wilful and comes from an intellectual pride which seeks to subvert the faith of others; the other is honest and comes from confusion – a disconnect between what one is expecting and what one experiences.

Even saints doubt. Here is St John Baptist, but we are also reminded of St Thomas. It is not fair that we should remember him as Doubting Thomas based on one moment in his life, for then we ought to call St John the Baptist, Doubting John, or St Peter, Denying Peter. If God put our sins away then most surely does He put away the frailties of His saints. Neither St John nor St Thomas sin for, when given the truth, they accept it gladly and go to their deaths with renewed vigour, preaching the Good News of Christ even by the shedding of their blood.

Two thousand years have passed and Christ has not yet come. This gives us confusion because we hear Him say that He will come again. The angels that announce His birth also announce that He will return in the same manner in which He ascended. We have every reason to doubt given that our experience and our expectations don't match. However, we are dealing with a real God Who will always go beyond our understanding and confuse it, just as our loved ones may catch us by surprise at times. We have a choice: we can disbelieve what God says and turn away into the first type of doubt, or we can continue our faith, knowing that we will be surprised by Love. The question we have to ask is whether or not we love God enough to trust Him.

Antiphon on Magnificat (Second Vespers)

Art Thou He † that should come, or do we look for another? Go and shew John those things which ye do see: the blind receive their sight, the dead are raised, and the poor have the Gospel preached unto them, alleluia.

Reflection

Doubt is dispelled by the evidence of our own experience or from people whose testimony we trust. Miracles are not something that can or should be repeated for God is not to be put to the test. From a Modern Scientific point of view, a happening that occurs only once and cannot be repeated or examined in full is dubious and often the eye-witnesses are assumed to have been mistaken with words such as, "people do not walk on water," or, "people do not rise from the dead." Miracles happen for our good, not to indulge our curiosity. God is not a lab rat!

And neither are we. Human beings are not the means to the end of understanding the Universe: human beings are ends in themselves as Immanuel Kant would himself bear witness. To apply scientific techniques to scientific questions will dispel scientific doubts. Each one of us has criteria by which we judge how convincing the evidence set before us is; those criteria will be personal to us even if the evidence is as objective as 2+2=4. Often this will give rise to cries of "gullible!" or "sceptic!" being bandied about pejoratively and thus denying each other the humanity that goes beyond labels.

Nonetheless, each one of us must accept the consequences of what we believe and these consequences will not always be pleasant: they will, of course, be utterly life changing. The more our beliefs are worth to us, then the longer we will hold onto them.

Monday

<u>*Antiphon on Benedictus*</u>

From heaven there cometh † the Lord, the Ruler, and in His hand are honour and dominion.

Reflection

The disconnect between expectation and experience is at its greatest when we see the Lord and Ruler from Heaven lying cooing in a manger rather than blasting into our small universe with all guns blazing and a myriad, myriad angels sounding a myriad, myriad golden trumpets. When we see the son of the carpenter, or perhaps construction worker, we wonder how this can be the Messiah, for kings and the sons of kings are to be found in palaces, not in the front room of a kinsman's house.

How can a little baby bear in its hand honour and dominion?

We might ask the same question of a baby Alexander the Great, or Julius Caesar. We won't know until it has grown up, surely?

And yet, we see that at the Epiphany to the magi who have seen the Star of Bethlehem in their charts and recognise the dominion of the baby and who thus honour Him with those famous three expensive gifts. We see God using even the profane pseudoscience of Astrology, (though yet still more noble than the star signs on the back pages of the tabloid newspaper) to make His revelation to those who seek the truth. This baby has altered things just by being born, even born into humble surroundings. This baby has come into being in the womb of a virgin. This baby has His life heralded by the angelic host. All these point to dominion beyond our thinking and which we only benefit from in hindsight.

However, we are still in Time's flux and we no longer have hindsight but must trust in the foresight of Holy Scripture and watch and wait for His coming again. The signs of that Second Advent will be there and, for the Faithful, they will be very apparent.

Antiphon on Magnificat

Behold the King shall come, † the Lord of the earth, and he shall take away the yoke of our captivity.

Reflection

The idea of a yoke is very powerful. We can see that our enslavement to sin forces us to walk along the same furrows again and again. We can see the patterns of our sin in our lives like the ridges in a ploughed field. Under a yoke, we may not turn even if we want to; we are forced to keep treading the same path without deviation while the fiend behind us gleefully cracks the whip as he sows more tares into the field which will yield the fruit of Death.

It is worth noting that some poor creatures will still tread the same path after being unyoked. They know no better, nor do they realise that the yoke has gone. This is very much the experience of many of us caught in habitual sin.

The difference is that the King comes not to yoke us and force us on our way, but yoke Himself to us. His yoke is easy because, although we may fall into the deep furrow of sin, He is still yoked to us and will always be with us whether we foolishly continue in sin, or turn to Him and beg Him to pull us out. He is yoked to us in our flesh and will not resign that yoke ever. Our Lord Jesus is always associated with our flesh and rejoices in it.

We are yoked to Him and so He is yoked to us in our death and we are yoked to Him in our resurrection. This is made all the more real at Mass. The priest remembers the yoke of Christ in putting on the Chasuble and thus binding himself to Christ the High Priest in the Lord's Supper. As the Mass continues, we are then presented with the Holy Sacrifice by which we are yoked to the whole Incarnation of Our Lord, become witnesses to the Crucifixion and receive the Body and Blood of Christ into ourselves. The Blessed sacrament fuses to our own bodies and our spirits, too, and thus provides a deeper and more binding yoke that the yoke of the flesh controlled by the forces of this dark world.

By the yoke of Christ, we will be yanked into Heaven with Him and thus be truly free of all the captivities of Hell.

Tuesday

Antiphon on Benedictus

The Lord shall arise upon thee, † O Jerusalem, and His glory shall be seen upon thee.

Reflection

There is within Classical Paganism an idea of the sleeping god. We see that with Elijah as the priests of Baal try to bring fire down from Heaven for their sacrifice and work themselves into a frenzy trying to wake the false god. Even today, we hear people say to us in our suffering, "shout louder, perhaps God might hear you!"

We still tell our children that, in the Evening, the Sun is going to bed and suggest that they might like to do the same. Yet, we have always known that the Sun continues its journey beyond the horizon and out of our sight. The Sun never sleeps, but moves on.

And the Lord Who keeps Israel slumbers not, nor sleeps. He is always awake and watching, though at times we simply cannot perceive His presence in the many and various Evenings in our souls, He is there and at work unseen, just as the Sun's warmth on the other side of the world still ensures that half the planet is not plunged into sub-zero temperatures but still sustains life.

We might be in the Night of our soul which we know to be long and dark. We watch and wait for the morning, not quite sure when the first rays of God's light will pour over the horizon, obliterating the gaudy neon lights of the world which try in vain to bring some light in the darkness.

We watch, and we wait, and soon, the Son of God shall rise.

Antiphon on Magnificat

The voice of one crying † in the wilderness, Prepare ye the way of the Lord, make straight in the desert a highway for our God.

Reflection

The practice in using the antiphons in the ferial office is to recite the antiphon up to the dagger, then say the Psalm or Canticle and, after the *Gloria Patri*, to say the antiphon in full. If today is a ferial day, then we begin with "The voice of one crying."

There are lots of voices crying out, and most are in pain and misery. How many times to our hearts break at the sight of another's suffering? How often are we tempted to turn our eyes away simply because we cannot bear the sorrow of our fellows?

The word "cry" has two meanings which we might see conflated here in the Advent of our God. We cry out in pain, and we cry out to announce. We know that pain and suffering are very much part of our existence and that pain and suffering are bound up in the sins of humanity.

As we learn to know God and to trust Him, then we realise that our cry of pain is not to Him: He already knows of our suffering and is doing something about it to the salvation of our souls in Eternity. It is our recognition of this that we cry out, not to God but to the world to prepare itself for Our Lord's ministry to humanity for its redemption from sin and death. Christians have always used their inevitable suffering for the benefit of the whole world in the Royal Priesthood of the Church. There is always an end to pain and suffering. They will pass with the Night, and joy will come in the Morning.

Wednesday

Antiphon on Benedictus

Behold I send my messenger, † and he shall prepare My ways before thy face.

Reflection

Why does God need to have His ways prepared? Why does He not just arrive?

One might think that our kings, queens and rulers need their ways prepared. The red carpet needs to be put out. The best dresses need to be put on. Everything needs to be spick and span for a Royal Visit. And the Ruler finds the reality of the host altered in order purely to impress. The dusty corners, the shabby drapery, the tired eyes caused by the late night and early morning, all are hidden away. Perhaps that is just what the Ruler wants. Perhaps the ability to cause this reaction in people reinforces that sense of control.

Yet, there is clearly a great opportunity for us to demonstrate our respect by responding with careful preparation to the announcement that we are to be visited by Royalty.

True Royalty comes from God. Our kings and queens, presidents and prelates are imperfect representations of the Kingship of God. Yet, we must remember that, in His love, He does not demand respect of anyone. The images that He uses of His coming is that of a wedding. He sends messengers to us to prepare for His coming so that we might be part of His celebrations. We have the opportunity to put our houses in order to participate in an event where we find ourselves confronted by the Perfect King and His Infinite regard for human beings. God is worthy of worship because of His utter regard for the integrity of Man as an autonomous being made lower than the angels to be crowned with glory and honour. We hold Him to the supreme worth because He first regards us as being worthy of Him. We love Him because He loves us first.

In giving us time to prepare, we can make our own decisions on how we come to approach Him. Those who love Him will fall upon their knees in adoration, and He will straighten them up and show them His love.

Antiphon on Magnificat

Sion, † thou shalt be renewed and shalt see thy righteous One, He that cometh unto thee.

Reflection

We look out onto a tired world. Into every aspect of our lives, discord is creeping. Scientists tell us that into every organised system entropy will increase and things will fizzle out. The current prediction of the end of the physical universe is that of a dark empty waste: no sun, no moon, no light; just isolated particles hanging in nothingness. Our tiredness comes from trying to hold things together against this tide of entropy – a battle of which Sisyphus would be proud.

As we see our politics descend into disarray, we might be tempted in our weary state to say, "Why bother?" Why bother in trying to uphold moral values when no-one listens? Why bother trying to protect the vulnerable when Society rides over you to get to them? Why bother in preaching a timeless faith when everyone else wants it altered to suit them?

In our tiredness, we can become prey to *acedia* – the monastic sin of sadness which results in asking, "Why bother?" and then just letting go.

We bother because God is. This is something the world wants us to forget and the Devil will take every opportunity to make what we do all about ourselves rather than about the worship of God.

What we do matters, even if we cannot perceive it. Saying our prayers day in, day out matters even if we are led to think no-one is listening. Praying that the suffering should recover even when they don't matter because it is the effort of love and the sufferer will be renewed when the Righteous One comes.

We cannot just regard Righteousness in legal terms. We have to see that when the Judge comes and judges each one of us, we will be made right. All the evil within us will be rooted out and done away with. Every hurt that we have suffered and every hurt that we have caused will be dealt with permanently. It will pain us because we will know what we have done but, in our renewal, we will be able to face it and know that what we see is our perfection in God.

Our judgment is coming and it will put us aright. Our God is coming and will not keep silent. Our God is coming, and so is our joy!

Thursday

Antiphon on Benedictus
Thou, O Lord, † art He that is to come, for Whom we look, to save Thy people.

Reflection
When faced with a personal problem, our typical reaction is to say, "I can do this myself! I can figure it out!" If it does get trickier, we might ask a friend to help us out. What we never do is step back and say, "You'll have to do this for me." In a professional life, we might "outsource" the areas in which we are least qualified to someone of the appropriate

skills. The fact that we use the phrase "outsource" instead of saying, "I can't do this. Would you do it for me?" demonstrates that we have a need not to be seen as incompetent.

To outsource a personal problem is something that fills us with revulsion. To do so would seem to be like asking Mummy to tie our shoe laces for us or to blow on our food. It is an affront to the person that we have become; it denies our status as an autonomous being.

One charge laid against Christianity is that it infantilises those who worship God. Often we hear people call our Faith a crutch for those who are weak to get someone to live their life for them. They see our prayers as pleas to the Universe to solve our problems for us. The fact is the Universe is indifferent to us.

Perhaps, when in difficulty and suffering, we do see Shadrach, Meshach and Abed-Nego unscathed and rejoicing in the burning fiery furnace and say, "why won't God do that for me in my problems? Why won't He heal me? Why won't He sort me out?" If we do, then perhaps we need to remember that God is not going to live our lives for us.

Yes, we are to put on Christ. Yes, it is not I that live but Christ that lives in me since I have been crucified with Christ. This is the point. The Christian accepts crucifixion - the sufferings of the life of Faith - willingly because the World needs its agony to be brought before God through the

Royal Priesthood of all Christians. The life of this world is nothing compared to the coming glory of Christ in Heaven. God may, for His own often unfathomable reasons, release us from the pain of our troubles as He has done in His miraculous works, but more suffering will come and so, in all probability, will death. Shadrach, Meshach and Abed-Nego all died, yet they live. In Christ we, too, rise and our sufferings will be no more.

Our life may be Christ's but we are still who we are and not somebody else. God created us to be the people we are and not puppets. We are children and not infants. Yet only He can save us, only He can create us and only He can raise us from the Dead. Only He can know and love us more than we know and love ourselves. We have to admit this, not to our shame, but in recognition that we are too powerless to save ourselves. Admitting this will not stop us from being who we are, but will set us free to become who we supposed to be.

Antiphon on Magnificat

He that cometh after me † is preferred before me, the latchet of Whose shoes I am not worthy to unloose.

Reflection

Self-worth is a minefield. It distorts our view of ourselves and the people around us if we don't get it right. There is a whole industry devoted to promoting and improving our sense of self-worth. Any distortion in our sense of self-worth can result in that form of idolatry called snobbery.

To be a snob, we have to have a way of comparing people in some respect. The people who are better than we are in that respect become the people we want to be; those who are worse than we are we look down upon and deride. There is even a sense of condescending pity on those who don't make the grade. "Poor them! They might still have valuable things to teach us, even if they are *technically* not really acceptable." There is even reverse snobbery in which we hate those whom we actually admire and consort with those who don't.

In either case, we are met with a form of self-loathing where we want to become someone we're not, or pull everyone "down" to our level. Or we can completely isolate ourselves from others. "No-one is as bad as I am," is the same as, "no-one is as good as I am." In both cases, the sense of self-worth is skewed away from what is healthy. We can do ourselves great hurt and both points of view need generous and careful treatment. The fact is that human beings are skewed by Evil and need love to bring them back to being healthy.

St John the Baptist knows how his sense of worth works. As far as he is concerned, any worth that he might have for himself must decrease so that his love of God may increase. He recognises that any worldly sense of status makes no sense when God arrives. He recognises that God is unapproachable. He knows that God is love and that he must return that love by putting God above all things, especially himself.

To the one who rejects God, this looks like self-loathing and, as we said earlier, may seek to treat St John for depression and lack of self-esteem. To St John, joy comes only in knowing God and playing a part in His Creation by rejecting the whole worldly system of self-worth as the rubbish that it is. All we need to know is that we are loved, that we have been made to be loved, and that one day, we will know that love in full.

Friday

Antiphon on Benedictus

Say to them: † Ye that are of a fearful heart, be strong: for behold the Lord Our God shall come.

Reflection

"Be not afraid!" the Angel says. Not easy to do when you're confronted by beings that you've always known about and yet never experienced. Everyone knows Angels are frightening to look at, but when you do see them, you forget that you don't have anything to worry about.

There are many things in this Earthly life that we're afraid of: spiders and snakes, prison and homelessness, pain and suffering, and Death. Can we be strong and not be afraid of them? Most of us will clearly need some help to confront the things that we are most afraid of. We need to understand why. Spiders and snakes may evoke race memories when these creatures posed a real threat to us. Prison and Homelessness play on our need for security, whilst the fear of pain and suffering speaks for itself. And the fear of Death. Does the Angel of Death tell us not to be afraid and be strong?

Coupled with Our Lord's advent as a baby in Bethlehem is our own advent before the judgement-seat of God where we face the Heavenly Host once more but in different circumstances. Whatever fears we may have on Earth, they are very, very temporary: what we face for Eternity is much scarier. As someone once said, "we are a long time dead." Facing God at His coming will indeed cause us to tremble and fall prostrate at His feet as though dead like St John in the first chapter of his Revelation. Yet God will set us on our feet by His strength and remind us that He is the Alpha and the Omega Who was dead and is now alive.

As we learn to trust Him in the strangeness and turbulence of Earthly life, so do we learn that our fear will be dispelled by His own hand. While His power and might will terrify us, He will still show us the baby in the manger and remind us that He is as small as we are and that we may share in being as great as He.

Antiphon on Magnificat

Sing unto the Lord † a new song: and His praise from the end of the earth.

Reflection

Christians are often accused of being Flat-Earthers despite good evidence to the contrary. Our view of reality is said to be against Science and against Reason. This is because, they say, that we are holding to an understanding of the world around us that is very old and therefore out-of-date. The world has moved on and scientific discoveries have made our ways of thinking obsolete.

But so much has not changed. Human beings, for all the technological advances still die. They still fight, wage wars, commit adultery and exhibit other behaviours that we still recognise as sin. Human philosophies have waxed and waned, governments have come and gone, and yet the question of God remains. Religions may rise and fall themselves, but religious belief has stood the test of time. Christianity is two-thousand years old and rests upon at least another two millennia of interaction with God in the Jewish religion.

The song that Christians sing comes from the beginning of Time. The tune may have changed a lot over that time, but the words are unmistakable: *Glory to God in the Highest and peace to His people on Earth.* We learned that from the Angels themselves. We have no issue with Science or Reason, indeed, the newness of Science and the deductions of Reason give us new ways to sing songs to God. Every scientific discovery affirms the glory of God rather than disconfirms His existence. Rather than view Science as being the end of our Faith, we need to use it to sing new, greater and deeper praises to the One from Whom all knowledge and wisdom flow.

Saturday

Antiphon on Benedictus

The Lord shall set up an ensign † for the nations, and shall assemble the outcasts of Israel.

Reflection

The ensign is the Cross – not the Star, nor the Manger, but the Cross. It is already prefigured in the gift of myrrh, in the deaths of the Holy Innocents and in the prophecy of the sword piercing Our Lady's soul. A simple enough design of two transverse lines it may be, but in them we see the heavens and Hades connected to the Horizon of the Earth.

And it is here that we who have been exiled from a life in God's presence will be drawn back to Him. Wherever we are at His coming, we will all meet at the foot of the Cross to ascend it and thus find our home with God once more. At the coming of Our King we will enter into the New Jerusalem to be part of His court once more. We will gather from the East and from the West and from the South, from the heights of the mountains, the depths of the sea, from the plains and the wildernesses, jungles and forests, from the living and the dead. No one can run from Him for even in Hades, He is there for us. He will always be for us, so who can be against us?

Third Sunday in Advent

Antiphon on Magnificat (First Vespers)

Before Me † there was no god formed, neither shall there be after Me: unto Me every knee shall bow, and Me shall every tongue confess.

Reflection

God speaks clearly of His majesty to the prophet Isaiah. Men worship many strange gods, even those that might not be recognisable as gods such as money, sex and power. He is very clear: He is God alone there is none beside Him.

The words the He uses are deliberately echoed by St Paul in his letter to the Church at Philippi and with which we are familiar in our hymn-singing. At the Name of Jesus, every knee shall bow. It is a clear statement not only that St Paul is confessing His belief that Our Lord Jesus is indeed God the Son, but that he is rehearsing a hymn that Christians were singing as he writes to the churches. This is sound biblical evidence that Our Lord Jesus is indeed God and is the only eternally begotten of the Father.

As we await His second Advent, we can rest assured that, though other religions may say that we worship many gods and others tell us that there is no God at all, we confess in our hearts, words and lives that there is but One in Three Persons.

Collect

Incline Thine ear to our prayers, O Lord, we beseech Thee; and lighten the darkness of our minds by the grace of Thy visitation, who with God the Father livest and reignest with the Holy Ghost, God throughout all ages, world without end. Amen.

Antiphon on Benedictus

He shall sit upon the throne † of David, and of His kingdom there shall be no end, alleluia.

Reflection

Again, we find ourselves faced with God Who breaks the walls of our understanding by standing inside and outside of His creation. We see successions of kings and queens stretching back through time. We see successions of bishops, too, each one passing on that Faith which we hold dear by their office if not by their lives and works.

Yes, bishops have oftentimes fallen short of the gravity of their office, neglected their duty sometimes grievously, and fallen far from the dignity of their calling. They are, however, held to account by the very faith that they are supposed to express and protect. Bishops and Monarchs alike may be held accountable to the oaths that they make to the people whom they serve.

Our Lord Jesus is the last of the line of kings coming from David, but He is the archetype of the priesthood in which bishops – and from them, priests – participate. He is the last of the kings and the first of the priests and yet, Time's End will be like Time's Beginning and He will be the first of kings and the last of priests. He is alpha and omega and in Him all will be fulfilled.

Antiphon on Magnificat (Second Vespers)

Blessed art thou, † O Mary, for thou hast believed the Lord: and there shall be a performance in thee of those things which were told thee from the Lord, alleluia.

Reflection

Faith matters. The very act of believing brings us in line with God. In order to believe, we must have something or someone to believe in and trust. In order to give us the gift of Faith, God gives us nothing less than Himself be it in the Garden, on Mount Sinai or Mount Horeb, be it in flood or still small voice. In order to have faith, we must be presented with it.

The dichotomy between faith and works is somewhat false as both aid each other. We are presented with faith as a gift, yet we have to open the present in order to receive it. For that, we need God's active presence with us, i.e. His grace.

Our Lady is presented with an object of faith – the angel whom she believes to be an angel based upon the revelation of God in the Old Testament. In receiving the angel, she is presented with his testimony which then makes the angel an object of faith in a different way, this time as a witness to the truth. She believes the angel and receives his words as being from God Himself. God now becomes the object of faith, and Our Lady's faith in Him grows ever deeper, so she says, "yes" to the uncertainty with which He presents her. And thus, as a result of these cycles of faith, Christ is born into the world and God Himself made manifest as an object of faith for us all which we may receive.

Faith is nothing if it is not received by activity. True faith can never be alone for it is always accompanied by actions of God and the one who cultivates faith. We never have faith once-for-all. What we do have is the life that God gives us to keep having and holding onto it through thick and thin. If our faith is alone, then we're not doing it right.

Monday

Antiphon on Benedictus

There shall come forth † a rod out of the stem of Jesse, and all the earth shall be filled with the glory of God: and all flesh shall see the salvation of God.

Reflection

"All flesh shall see the salvation of God." What does that mean?

It means something more than perhaps we have hitherto understood. St Luke could have said, "The Elect shall see the salvation of God." Yet, it is all *flesh*- all humanity – that shall see the salvation of God. That doesn't mean to say that all humanity will receive salvation, but rather that it will recognise salvation when the Earth is filled with the Glory of God.

So why do human beings not perceive salvation now? The Angels sang, "Glory to God in the Highest!" and His glory shone around the shepherds abiding in the fields. The Magi perceive the star of the Messiah in the Eastern sky and recognise that. Still, this little group of people whom we find represented in the Nativity Scene surely doesn't form all mankind.

It may not form all mankind, but it is an ikon of all mankind.

Whilst God bears our image, He is as localised and as small as we are. The human eye cannot behold any larger; the human heart is not yet ready to love; the human mind cannot yet comprehend salvation. When we are ripe for the harvest, then we shall see the glory of God and then we shall truly see what salvation is.

What we shall see is all Creation purged of Evil, all harms healed, all wrongs righted and those who reject God given precisely what they want in the outer darkness away from His glory.

However, there is no single human being to whom salvation will not be offered.

Antiphon on Magnificat
All generations † shall call me blessed: for God hath regarded the lowliness of His handmaiden.

Reflection

This is a great truth, for only those who will not see refuse to call the Virgin Mary blessed. Yet, she is blessed by God. She does not earn her blessing, but rather she enters into the blessing that she receives. The blessing of the Christ-Child within her is not an easy thing: why do we think that blessings have to be comfortable?

It is an unfortunate thing that we think that there is an equivalence between being happy and being blessed. Indeed the Greek word for blessing is often translated by "happy." The trouble is that happiness is an accident of circumstance. We are happy when we find an extra chocolate biscuit in a packet, that we have one the lottery or when we have missed catching a cold.

A blessing comes from God and changes the way we see happiness. Mary, a young virgin, betrothed to be married, is blessed with the Holy Baby despite the damage it would do to her reputation. We can imagine a girl of her age falling pregnant and receiving a lot of unpleasantness as a result. The blessing Our Lady receives contains a sword that will pierce her soul – how can that be happy? Yet, she is willing to receive it, and the end of this blessing is her crown in Heaven. To be associated with God does not come from chance, and yet it incorporates true happiness that will last for Eternity.

Tuesday

<u>Antiphon on Benedictus</u>

Thou, Bethlehem, † in the land of Juda, shalt not be the least: for out of thee shall come a Governor, that shall rule my people Israel.

Reflection

We must not despise the day of small things. The fact that our sense of value and worth is distorted means that we have to be careful about the reasons we accept or reject things. Bigger does not necessarily mean better. We already see little David conquer massive Goliath with a tiny stone and one man defeat an entire army with the jawbone of an ass.

One thing we have, perhaps, forgotten how to do is to see worth and value in everything that we perceive for the simple reason that God put it there. This is a goal worth striving for because the goal is the fullest worship of God we can muster. We have a little baby in a little manger in a little room of a little house in the little town of Bethlehem who will change the world. The butterfly will flap its wings in Nazareth and the world will change in the resulting storm. In just a little while and He shakes the Heaven, the Earth, the Sea, the dry land and all nations.

However, the storm will be over when He comes to reign in Peace and our sense of true worth will be restored.

Antiphon on Magnificat

Awake, awake, † arise, O Jerusalem: loose thyself from the bands of thy neck, O captive daughter of Sion.

Reflection

Are we to loose ourselves from our sins? This seems to be what God tells Isaiah. Does this mean that we can save ourselves?

God presents us with a choice. The fact of the matter is that He has indeed unlocked the shackles that bind us and that He wants us to see that this is precisely what He has done. How foolish then it would be just to sit in our prison in our chains rather than pull them off from us! And yet this is what we do.

God wants our freedom to be His Creation. He created us to be and to do, to will and to reason, to build and to sing. We are not to be passive.

Neither are we what we do. There is a distinction. We are not to allow ourselves to be constrained by artificial concepts but rather by the truth that God reveals to us. We are male and female as God made us – other than that, we are to become whom God created us to be and released from the prison of sinful and earthly ideologies. Too often we shackle ourselves to our jobs or to our lifestyles believing that these are who we are. And so when we are released from them by the Divine Hand, we fail to remove their shackles from us.

We need to wake up to the fact that reality is not what we want it to be. It belongs to God and so do we.

Ember Wednesday

Antiphon on Benedictus

The Angel † Gabriel was sent to Mary, a Virgin espoused to Joseph.

Reflection

And this is where the Old Testament comes to its end. It's a strange thought that, although the Gospels form the beginning of the New Testament, the New Testament doesn't begin until the Crucifixion and the spilling of the blood of Christ for our sake. St John the Baptist, Zachariah, Elizabeth, the child-murdering Herod, even St Joseph are all Old Testament figures. The first figures of the New Testament are Our Lady and Our Lord.

Our Lady is unique in that she truly spans both testaments because she is true to both testaments. She keeps the old Law and receives the covenant in the blood of her son. She is a figure of the dawn of mankind's ascent to God in opposition to the Eve of mankind's fall from God.

While she may form the centre pages between the two testaments, it is Christ Our Lord who staples them together through the Blessed Virgin. She is the instrument of His work, not a co-worker. Yet, she becomes an illuminated manuscript of the best kind forever pointing to the Son of God through the colour of her life and being. The pages of

Holy Scripture hold so many ikons who illuminate the way to Our Lord, yet He is the One who holds them and us and God together.

Collect

Grant, we beseech Thee, Almighty God: that the upcoming festival of our redemption may bring us aid in this present life, and bounteously bestow the rewards of eternal blessedness. Through Jesus Christ, Thy Son, Our Lord, who liveth and reigneth with Thee in the unity of the Holy Ghost, God, world without end. Amen

Antiphon on Magnificat

Behold the handmaid of the Lord; † be it unto me according to thy word.

Reflection

We might like to think that we say this to God, but we don't. There are times when we do what we love doing and say that we do it for God.

There are times when we are bidden to do work that we find tiresome for the sake of God. There are times when we must also just stand still and wait to be called. Our duty is to do as we are told and if it means being bored or doing something revolting, then we must do it.

In circumstances like these, it is often difficult to see the love that God has for us and to feel the love that we have for God. It may well be that our love for God is love for a god who will let us do just what we want to do. That is not God – unless, of course, our will is so perfectly aligned to His which, given the nature of our fall seems unlikely. Often the god that commands us to enjoy ourselves always in whatever we decide to do is not the God that we want to love. It is hard for us to discern His will which is why the command to stand and wait is so beneficial for us as we learn to listen carefully and hear truly what He wants us to do.

Our Lady risks her reputation, her health and her life and then seems to spend the Gospels hovering around in the background watching what her son will say and do. After His ascension, she lives with St John and simply tells people her story about the Truth. This is what we should be doing.

Thursday

Antiphon on Benedictus
Be ye watchful † in your hearts, for the Lord our God is nigh at hand.

Reflection
Being on watch is a difficult thing. Somehow, we have to be vigilant and wait for things to happen, and yet our minds wander and distractions set in. Yes, we can physically be in the watchtower, but our minds can be elsewhere. We are not fully present at our watch, just partly there like a reverse ghost. While the ghost is the disembodied spirit, so the wandering mind causes us to be like a dispirited body. If our

prayer is just time spent reading the words whilst the mind is contemplating the tasks of the day then we are not fully present to God.

Our duty is to be fully present at our watch and this means training our minds to focus on the task in hand. We have to want to be present and take our Christian duties to heart. The activity of being Christian helps us avoid being caught unawares by the sudden return of the King.

The Lord is not just nigh at hand in His return, He is also nigh to our hearts in which He may freely gaze and see us in our entirety. While our minds may wander during our prayers, there is still the fact that something in us wants to be saying them even if our minds are a million miles away. That something resides in the heart of us: we know it to be right to pray; we know it to be good and restorative. We gain, however, the fullest benefit when we rein in our thoughts like errant dogs on leashes for then we can be nigh unto God in the entirety of our being.

Antiphon on Magnificat

Rejoice ye † with Jerusalem; and be glad with her, all ye that love her, forever.

Reflection

These days, we look at Jerusalem with mixed feelings given the stormy history she has, especially from the mid-Twentieth Century. She does not quite appear as a city where much rejoicing happens given the unease and strife that has taken place over the centuries. She has been "loved" by many people trying to possess her and claim her for their own. She has been enslaved by many an empire and the fractures in her society are always very delicate.

To love means to set the beloved free. This is what God has done for us. He has set us free from the obligation to worship Him like an automaton and seeks to enflame us with the desire to worship Him of our own freewill. Yet, the Fall from God has made humanity as fractured as Jerusalem. We, too, have suffered many enslavements of our souls and spirits from infernal forces. Ours is a stormy history of which Jerusalem stands as a microcosm and synecdoche.

In watching with St John the Divine and seeing the New Jerusalem coming out of Heaven, we realise our own destiny. If Jerusalem is to be renewed and transformed then so may we. If Jerusalem in her troubles may rejoice in her salvation then so may we. If Jerusalem can receive her saviour at His presentation in the temple then we, too, may receive Him in the temple of our own selves at our presentation to Him through the waters of our Baptism.

We are inextricably linked with Jerusalem and we should pray for her peace, for in doing so we shall prosper in loving her.

Ember Friday

Antiphon on Benedictus

For lo, † as the voice of thy salutation sounded in mine ears, the babe leaped in my womb for joy, alleluia.

Reflection

It's a wonderful feeling for the mother when she first feels the tiny flutter heralding the life of the baby within her. It is just as wonderful for the father when the baby responds to his voice. The father can never experience what it is to bear another human being within his body – it is a privilege solely reserved for mothers, but so is the travail of birth!

How must it feel for the baby, snug, warm and in a strange darkness, when he hears a voice that it recognises speaking words of love? To recognise someone whom you have never seen is remarkable. How more remarkable to hear the voice of someone who carries within her the One Who Knows each one of us more intimately than we know ourselves. Just as the mother cannot know the inside of her ow body, neither can we know the inside either of our bodies or of our souls.

Yet, St John the Baptist shows that we will know God even if our eyes have never beheld Him. We will know Him because He will know us and we will know that we are known. As our earthly life is filled with our travail against our sins and shortcomings as well as enduring those of others, so can we bring to birth within ourselves a greater recognition of the One Who Is. Like the baby still in formation in the mother's womb, so are we in formation in the Spirit until we are born again at our death to this world. Even before this birth, we can still recognise the voice of our Saviour and leap for joy!

Collect

Stir up Thy might, we beseech Thee, O Lord, and come: that we who put our trust in Thy goodness may speedily be delivered from all adversity. Who with God the Father, in the unity of the Holy Ghost livest and reignest, God, throughout all ages, world without end. Amen.

Antiphon on Magnificat

This is the witness † which John bare, saying: He that cometh after me is preferred before me.

Reflection

The strange fact of the Incarnation of Our Lord is that the One to Whom Time is subordinate enters into its flow. He Who is at the Beginning and at the End in His Divinity suffers beginning and end in His Humanity. St John the Baptist is older than Our Lord, but He is not His elder. No prophet will be greater than St John but he is surpassed by the least in the kingdom of God.

St John is content with this status. It renders all the quibbles of comparing the self with others completely worthless. There is no need to chase the ghosts of departed elitism and so the soul is liberated from the need to chase after such baubles and trinkets. On the ground, there is nowhere to fall. And on the ground is where God walks with us.

Ember Saturday

Antiphon on Benedictus

How shall this be, † O Angel of God, seeing I know not a man? Hearken, O Virgin Mary: the Holy Ghost shall come upon thee, and the power of the Highest shall overshadow thee.

Reflection

Why is virginity so prized? Surely, the whole business of parenthood is holy and noble. Marriage is a sacred estate attested to by St Paul.

Virginity is not for everyone, otherwise the human race would cease to be. However, Virginity points to chastity and a powerful stand against the lusts of the flesh. Virginity allows for a peculiar devotion to God and for Our Lady, this Virginity demonstrates clearly the Jesus Christ is the Son of God.

Of course, there will be those who develop unhealthy interests in disparaging Our Lady's status as the Blessed Virgin Mother of God. In her day, her honour is questioned so as to deny Our Lord's Divine Origin. In this day, her honour is questioned so as to give some justification for the promiscuity of those who prefer their gratification to the worship of God.

Those who consecrate their virginity to God find themselves in the company of Our Lady. Those who commit to the sanctity of Marriage also find themselves in the company of Our Lady for her fidelity to both God and St Joseph shines brightly. Thus the Virgin Mother consecrates in herself to her Son all who seek to live in holy chastity.

Collect

O God, Who seest that we are afflicted through our own perverseness: mercifully grant that we may be comforted by Thy visitation. Who with God the Father, in the unity of the Holy Ghost livest and reignest, God, throughout all ages, world without end. Amen.

Fourth Sunday in Advent

From this Sunday, the Antiphon on the Magnificat will always be one of the Great O Antiphons which are dealt with separately.

Antiphon on Benedictus

Hail Mary, † thou that art full of grace, the Lord is with thee; blessed art thou among women, alleluia.

Reflection

If no less than the angel of the Lord feels compelled to salute Mary then it stands to reason that we should too. As we approach the Feast of the Nativity, we must be aware that Our Lady is not only full of grace in her soul but also in her body, for she bears the Christ-child and there can be no more an obvious expression of the active presence of God.

It is not for us to know Our Lady's experience of this pregnancy. The humanity of Our Lord does point to it being a human pregnancy; the Divinity of Our Lord reminds us not to be so sure. As a mother near the time of her delivery becomes more uncomfortable, so we may too become uncomfortable in not quite knowing what to expect. Some will say that Our Lady's sinlessness will mean that she is excused the pain of childbirth inherited by sinful Eve. Others will say that the humanity of both Lord and Lady will mean that the birth has no reason to be different from any other child. Our reason may jostle between the two positions. Yet there is one certainty: Christ is to be born.

Collect

Stir up Thy power, we beseech Thee, O Lord, and come: and with great might succour us, that with the help of Thy grace that which is hindered by our sins may be hastened by Thy merciful forgiveness. Who with God the Father, in the unity of the Holy Ghost livest and reignest, God, throughout all ages, world without end. Amen.

Monday

Antiphon on Benedictus

Thus saith the Lord † your God: Repent ye, and turn again; for the kingdom of heaven is at hand, alleluia.

Reflection

"Repent" is the first word that we hear from Our Lord as He comes out of the obscurity of his formative years and into His public ministry. Given that the word means to change one's mind, to say "repent and turn" seems almost unnecessary. What we do know from bitter experience that often when we think we have repented from a sin, we relapse almost immediately. It is as if we think we have turned ourselves fully to God when in reality we have merely glanced in His direction. True repentance is hard because it involves a turning of the whole self from sin.

In talking of the capricious nature of the tongue, St James reminds us that a small rudder can turn a whole ship. Yet, this reminds us that there is something that we can do to ensure that we repent more fully of our sins and this involves knowledge of our moral compass that ensures control of our direction towards God. The rudder that keeps straight will not turn the ship at all; the rudder that is fixed in one direction will drive the ship in circles. We need to be sure that once we have sight on Christ as Polaris, we must keep our eyes and our heart fixed on Him. Prayer, fasting and the study of the wisdom to be found in Holy Scripture and the Church Fathers will help us keep our direction.

Tuesday

Antiphon on Benedictus

Awake, awake, † put on strength, O arm of the Lord

Reflection

This arm of the Lord is a figure of Jerusalem whom Isaiah beseeches to hear the voice of God throughout the fifty-first chapter of his prophecy. Why should Jerusalem put on strength?

The prophet Isaiah reminds Jerusalem of her flight from Egypt through the waters of the sea and how the Lord triumphed gloriously. This is a call to have faith and to be comforted – strengthened.

And Jerusalem is a figure for the Church and for our human lives which are afflicted by sin and death. In times of darkness and struggle, we are to look to the Lord. We are to look back on His triumphs on our behalf, how He saves us in the words of the Old Testament, and how He still saves us in the words of the New. Of course, this seems all so long ago for us twenty centuries distant. We fear that this is all so long ago that it is too shrouded in myth to be any comfort to us. Yet, the person of Jesus Christ is there in History as surely as Caesar, Socrates and Confucius. The Gospels are eye-witness statements that record these facts and the lives of the saints still testify to this strong and active God.

We need to awaken to the reality of God, and Christmas Day is as much of a testament to this reality through its yearly celebration since that great day!

Wednesday

Antiphon on Benedictus
I will place salvation † in Sion, and in Jerusalem my glory, alleluia.

Reflection
Bethlehem is about half-an-hour's drive from Jerusalem, i.e. about seven miles away, so is easily walkable in the space of a few hours. Nazareth, on the other hand, is about sixty miles to the North of Bethlehem as the crow flies, but the road is about ninety miles and thus three or four days' journey on foot on a fairly arduous route.

We can imagine this being a rather perilous journey for one as great with child as Our Lady as she embarks to fulfil the requirements of the census. Still, though, she is obedient and in her obedience, she fulfils the Lord's prophecy for our Salvation is born on the outskirts of Jerusalem, will preach in Jerusalem, be crucified and die outside the walls and will present His risen self once more inside the city. Further, He will present the New Jerusalem as the Bride of Christ – the Holy Catholic Church – as the place where His salvation may be found. We, too, must journey through a perilous route in order to get there, but Christ has trodden this road before and continues to walk with us to its glorious end.

Thursday

Antiphon on Benedictus
Comfort ye, † comfort ye my people, saith your God

Reflection
If we have regarded Advent as a penitential season then we may well find ourselves somewhat weakened by our fasting, especially in a society which has been celebrating Christmas since November. The sight of all the Christmas food in the shops, offers and discounts from various emporia and the emphasis on presents and food from every quarter of social media can be very wearing to the one practising a principled Christian ascesis.

Our season of penitence brings us into solidarity with those encumbered by the darkness of the soul and for whom the struggle to celebrate anything is great. Our Christian priesthood bids us consecrate human suffering to God so that it might become holy and thus receive a dignity that passes the irrelevance of materialistic celebration.

As we come to the end, we hear the prophet's words telling us that we are ever nearer to the light and that we have every reason to summon strength for the finish line. Our comfort of receiving the infant Christ into our arms promises the comfort for every suffering soul in the arms of Christ.

Friday

Antiphon on Benedictus
Behold all things are fulfilled † which were spoken by the Angel of the Virgin Mary

Reflection
We reach the fulfilment of Our Lady's annunciation. Daily, Catholics around the world remember this in the recitation of the *Angelus* three times a day – morning, noon and evening.

In the morning, the *Angelus* reminds us of that annunciation and the proclamation of the prophecy of Our Lady. At noon, the *Angelus* serves to cause us to pause in the middle of our journey to give us comfort in the continuation of our work. And now, as we reach Advent's evening, with the goal in sight, we remember say the *Angelus* for the third time waiting for Christ's light to shine in the darkness of the night.

Here we are, our journey nearly over, our fasts complete, and our hope imminent. And we find ourselves back at the beginning, once more remembering the visit of the Angel to Our Lady, and yet finding ourselves enriched by the presence of the One Who is always new by virtue of His Eternity. The cycle begins again, not in monotony but spiralling upwards, ever upwards to the Divine.

The Great Advent Antiphons on the Magnificat

December 16th

Antiphon on Magnificat

O Wisdom, † which camest out of the mouth of the Most High, and reachest from one end to another, mightily and sweetly ordering all things: Come and teach us the way of prudence.

Reflection

Philosophers debate what it means to know something and, indeed, whether it is possible to know something truly. All that we know seems fleeting. We forget easily, or misremember what it is we are supposed to know. Other things seem past our understanding and we draw false conclusions from vague shadows. What is this Wisdom that comes out of the mouth of God?

Is this the same Wisdom that is "created in the beginning" and shall never fail, or is this something deeper given that it proceeds directly out of the mouth of God Himself? Is this not the Spirit of Wisdom and Understanding which is possessed by the Messiah?

Here we see the procession of the Holy Ghost deriving His substance from the Father, the Eternal Source of Light Divine. We are told of, though we do not comprehend, the origin of the Holy Ghost as we consider the birth of Our

Lord. Both have their origin in the Father, and the Father only becomes a Father when He has begotten His Son: He only becomes a source when the Spirit has proceeded forth from Him.

The Holy Persons of the Trinity are more intimately bound to each other than we can ever hope to know: their being is but One which can never be said for humans – a One that is not solitary. And yet, with the wisdom that they pour into the world, we have the invitation to participate. We receive Wisdom through a gift of the Holy Ghost by which we gain glimpses into what truly is. Our knowledge is only in part; our wisdom is only in part, but the part vanishes when the wholeness comes. What we claim to know on Earth is only a shadow of the truth. Really, the thing we call "knowledge" is a series of deepening beliefs based on what is revealed to us. Soon, we shall know nothing at all, because we shall know God and that will be true knowledge.

December 17th

Antiphon on Magnificat

O Adonai, † and Leader of the house of Israel, Who appearedst in the bush to Moses in a flame of fire, and gavest him the Law in Sinai: Come and redeem us with an outstretched arm.

Reflection

In the fire of God's righteousness, we see what is righteous described in the Law and handed to Moses. Here we are shown what is right and what is wrong and we understand that right and wrong to be aspects of Who God is and Who He is not. We are also shown that pure goodness can pour forth from created things and not consume them: the mercy of God comes from His self-limitation so that we sinful, foolish beings endowed with His image, may not be lost. The giving of the Law is accompanied by the fire of the Holy Ghost which seeks entry into the heart. Yet the hearts of men are bound up tight and locked by sin.

This pure goodness comes forth from a pure Virgin. God limits Himself once more only this time as a human being. Yet, this human body is not created as we are. This human body is a direct result of God's limitation just as God's glory is limited to the bush so that a man may gaze upon it. This is the body whose heart will be broken so that ours may be broken. The Spirit that pours out from the pierced heart will poor into ours when it is broken and contrite.

Again, we see the complexity of the Holy Trinity intertwine with humanity for our redemption. Both Son and Spirit are propelled into our lives by the arm of God stretched out to judge and to pull us out of judgement. Mercy and Justice in God are combined whereas in our human frailty we perceive them as opposites, just as we get obsessed with the idea of being either a victim or a perpetrator of crime.

In God, we see that we are both victim and transgressor. In God we see that He is Justice and Mercy.

December 18th

Antiphon on Magnificat

O Root of Jesse, † Which standest for an ensign of the people, at Whom kings shall shut their mouths, unto Whom the Gentiles shall seek: Come and deliver us, and tarry not!

Reflection

Again we are drawn back to the Cross of Christ as the wood of Jesse is nailed to the wood of the Earth standing like the golden serpent in order to cure humanity of the curse of sin and death.

It is the Cross that makes the leaders of the nations stand silenced in astonishment. How can a device of torture become a symbol of hope? How can the death of one man inspire so many to die in the belief of new life? How can the birth of a baby so many years distant still influence so many even if we cannot be sure when he was born nor where in Bethlehem?

While many still argue over Christmas, its very presence in the memory of our society still marks it out as a special time. It is true that it is covered up in the tinsel of paganism and mammon, but at its heart, beyond the pagan devotion to the solstice and the means of a quick buck, the Nativity is still there. Saint Nicholas is still a person of history like his master, the Christ-Child.

People are indeed astonished that, in this day of reason and science, there are those who hold to older and deeper truths inaccessible to the hardened heart. Perhaps their astonishment may turn to awe and wonder.

December 19th

Antiphon on Magnificat

O Key of David, † and Sceptre of the house of Israel; that openest, and no man shutteth; Who shuttest and no man openeth: Come and bring the prisoners out of the prison-house that sit in darkness and the shadow of Death.

Reflection

Why David's key? Why not Adam's or Abraham's? Or God's?

We know that Our Lord is born of this thread of history known as the Root of Jesse to its eternal fulfilment. Isaiah prophesies to the key of David being on the shoulder of the Messiah. This is the Key to the City of David, the New Jerusalem which St John sees coming out of Heaven adorned as a bride for her husband. Our Lord is the Key to this City; He is the Way in and the Door. We cannot enter the city of God except through Christ and none else.

And look what happens.

The Keys to the Kingdom of Heaven are given to St Peter. Here we see the transfer of God's grace from the Kings and Prophets of the Old Testament to the priests and bishops of the New. As Christ becomes the Pontiff – the bridge between Heaven and Earth – so He opens His role to those whom He ordains as His priests. The Church possesses the keys to Heaven. The Keys to Hell, however, are given to an Angel in the Revelation.

This is something we must consider carefully. It is the vocation of the Church to draw people in to the City of David through the exercise of Christ's love and grace. We have nothing to do with Hell and the Second Death. Let others worry about that while we fix our gaze upon the Way to God.

December 20th

Antiphon on Magnificat

O Day-spring, † Brightness of the Light everlasting, and Sun of Righteousness: come and enlighten them that sit in darkness and the shadow of Death.

Reflection

Of course, with the benefit of telescopes we know full well that the Day-spring – the Morning Star – is the planet Venus sailing through the void on an orbit closer to the Sun than ours. It often seems that scientific reasoning destroys poetry and metaphor. Our Ancestors did not have access to the technological revolution through which we have passed. It's easy for us to say that, because the Ancients did not know about the true nature of planets, their access to the truth is suspect and their testimony to be taken with a pinch of salt. There is a snobbery in modern thinking that all truth known of old must pass the test of modern methods to be true. We can be so patronising with human beings who are so long dead that even their disciples' disciples cannot defend them. The result is that knowledge is lost, like the reason for building Stonehenge.

We can and should rely on scientific discovery to inform us about the world around us, but recognise that there can and must be limits to what we can know through the study of the universe – our science points precisely to the existence of truth inaccessible to human reason. This is why the truth has to be revealed to us. We know only of the birth of Christ because the angels told us that He was to be born. Celestial Mechanics may have pointed the Magi to a child born in Bethlehem but finding the child in the town was not to be an easy job – why else would Herod have issued his terrible order? Star-charts could only tell them so much. Surely they will have come across the testimony of one to whom the angels appeared.

We rely on an Enlightenment from beyond Creation in order to see the Holy Uncreate. The Enlightenment of Human Reason might have allowed us to see more of Creation, but it has darkened our understanding of things Divine. Sometimes, we just have to put aside our instruments and charts, and learn to pray.

December 21ˢᵗ

Antiphon on Magnificat

O King of the Nations † and their Desire; the Cornerstone, who makest both one: Come and save mankind, whom Thou formedst of clay.

Reflection

A corner is where two walls meet and the stone at the corner sets the pattern for that meeting. A cornerstone made out of clay would crack and crumble the moment a sufficient weight is put upon it. We see the statue of Nebuchadnezzar's dream crumble with its feet of clay.

If Christ is the corner stone, and we are things of clay, then how can He truly share human nature? Stone and clay are not the same.

We see here that the promise of Christ is quite clear: we are to be transformed. Our Lord looks at St Peter and calls him Rock and it is upon the rock of Peter's confession of faith as St John Chrysostom reminds us, and therefore that same confession of the other disciples that the Church is to be built. We become rock by taking the substance of Christ. It is through the Holy Sacrament that we become the building of the Church and our transformation is completed only in Christ.

This is why we long for Him. Our nature is so fragile, friable and fallible that those who recognise it yearn for completeness which can only come at the hands of God and not of any work of ours.

December 22nd

Antiphon on Magnificat

O Emmanuel, † our King and Lawgiver, the Desire of all nations and their salvation: Come and save us, O Lord, Our God.

Reflection

The Law that Emmanuel gives is something we have known about for centuries before He comes forth from the virgin's womb. The fallenness of Humanity means that we have been broken by trying to bear the Law. This is ironic, because we know the Law has no weight, no power, no grasp over those who are truly righteous and do good from the heart. Neither has it power to save those who transgress it.

What is this Law? Another irony. This is the knowledge of Good and Evil whose fruit the Man and the Woman believed that they could consume in the Garden. As a result of this sin, death enters the world and, with death, a fissure throughout human nature. As a cracked stone can no longer bear the full weight of its former burden, likewise our human nature cannot bear the weight of the Law.

Only the Cornerstone and His Divine Humanity can rectify this through the salvation that He offers. We shall be like Him for we shall see Him as He really is, and then righteousness will be in our human nature for we shall share His Divine nature. The Law shall pass away, but the Word of God shall not pass away.

December 23rd

Antiphon on Magnificat

O Virgin of virgins, † how shall this be? For neither before thee was any seen like thee, nor shall there be after. Daughters of Jerusalem, why marvel ye at me? The thing which ye behold is a divine mystery.

Reflection

Our focus on Christ appears to be interrupted as we turn, so near to Christmas, to Our Lady. Many would object: Our Lord is surely the centre of our devotion and worship at this time. We must not worship Mary.

Yet, as the Child begins its arduous journey into the world, where can we look but to the Mother? Immediately before birth, all eyes must be for the Mother in her travail and difficulty. It is from her that the Child will emerge into the cold world from the warmth of the womb. It is to her breast that the Child will cling and gain sustenance.

With the birth of Our Saviour a day away, we must look to the Theotokos in due reverence and veneration as she brings to us Our Lord Jesus Christ. And where she is, He is never far away. And where He is, she is close at hand. This is not worship of Mary, it is due gratitude, just as we ought to have for our own mother for bringing us into the world.

She will be with this baby all His life and do her duty in bringing Him up while pondering His miraculous life in her heart. How full of grace is her life!

Vigil of the Nativity

Antiphon on Benedictus

The Saviour † of the world shall arise as the sun: and shall come down into the Virgin's womb, as the showers upon the grass, alleluia.

Reflection

It seems a little paradoxical for the Lord to be compared with both sunshine and showers and yet these form the perfect conditions for the presence of a rainbow. The rainbow is God's promise to Noah of the covenant that He wants with sinful humanity.

We now see with our own eyes and our own hearts the fulfilment of that promise and the refreshing of the covenant so that we can still hope for the things that we may not yet see with added vigour.

Tomorrow, we see more promises fulfilled and yet more given to our salvation and our glorification in Him. This is the faithfulness of God to us. This is our destiny. This truly is worth celebrating!

Collect

O God, Who makest us glad with the yearly expectation of the birth of Thine only Son Jesus Christ: grant that as we joyfully receive Him for our Redeemer, so we may with confidence behold Him when He shall come to be our Judge. Who with Thee, in the unity of the Holy Ghost liveth and reigneth, God, throughout all ages, world without end. Amen.

Feast of the Nativity

Antiphon on Magnificat (First Vespers)

When the sun hath risen † in the heavens, ye shall see the King of kings proceeding from the Father, as a bridegroom out of His chamber.

Reflection

Weddings these days are nerve-wracking affairs. Everything has to be right. You can see the bride and her entourage fussing about making sure that every last detail is correct. And the groom?

Popular culture seems to present the groom nervously worrying whether he has done the right thing, whether he is marrying the right person, whether she is the girl for him.

What does it say, then, if the groom bursts forth from his room, properly attired with an air of triumph and bursting with confidence? What a bride she must be to have such an effect on her intended spouse. How he must love her, and how happy she will be to have a husband who is so confident in his love for her.

This is the joy of the Church, for her Bridegroom is unerring and more constant than the risen sun in His regard for her. See how He disregards the fallen nature of humanity and expresses this certainty of love by becoming attired in the flesh of Man. His betrothal to the Church is absolute and He will be a husband for whom there can be no match in perfection.

Collect

Grant, we beseech Thee, Almighty God, that the new birth in the flesh of Thine only-begotten Son may deliver us; who are held fast in the old bondage under the yoke of sin. . Through the same Jesus Christ, Thy Son, Our Lord, who liveth and reigneth with Thee in the unity of the Holy Ghost, God, world without end. Amen

Antiphon on Benedictus

Glory † to God in the highest, and on earth peace to men of good will, alleluia, alleluia.

Reflection

And so it comes to pass that human beings can join in the song of the angels. We have learned the words and there are now so many wonderful musical settings of these words which speak of the unification of Earth and Heaven through the birth of the infant God.

Our voices will be low and earthy in comparison to the air-like quality of the angels' notes. Our instruments are cumbersome in comparison to the bright sounds of the angel trumpets. Yet we will all be singing the same song – not in unison, but in a rich harmony for the same song can be enriched by different layers of notes.

Every Christmas carol that we sing from the heart fits with that glorious song in ways that earthly music cannot. It is only when we are in the presence of God that we can hear this song of heaven and earth combined. For Isaiah, it is that glorious seraphic cry of "Holy, Holy, Holy" before the throne of God. For us, it is "Glory to God in the Highest" before the manger holding the tiny baby.

Antiphon on Magnificat (Second Vespers)

To-day † the Christ is born; to-day hath a Saviour appeared: to-day on earth Angels are singing. Archangels rejoicing: to-day the righteous exult and say, Glory to God in the highest, alleluia.

Reflection

There comes a moment in the maternity ward where all is still. The labour is over; all are cleaned up and beginning to relax. The tiny child is at the breast for the first time. And it is as if Time itself stops. There is relief and joy as eyes meet for the first time and the crying subsides. There is silence, but it is a silence filled with unheard noises of euphoria and pure jubilation.

What we see now is a foretaste of our destiny. The infant Jesus already tears open the veil to reveal Eternity itself. Our Lord shows us that human birth is a foretaste of Heaven itself, filled with relief and joy as sins are obliterated and pain quenched. Our eyes meet with God's in this strange recognition, and all our weeping ceases as the Divine hand wipes the tears from our eyes.

It is true that, for us all, life must run its course. Babies grow up and the realities of living hit them, sometimes hard. In this life, beginnings have endings and there is always pain and sorrow. The Baby in the manger will, in the eyes of the unbelieving, come to a terrible end. In the eyes of History, this death is not the end and the Resurrection will staple History to Eternity.

And we, who have the opportunity to stand with Him in Eternity will know the worth of the pain of living and the joy that comes from it as Death is abolished. We cannot understand this profound reality now for we are merely infants in the eyes of God. We are creatures in Time who are promised to be free from Time by the Holy Infant Himself. We can only live in to-day.

But to-day is The Day! This is the day that the Lord has made. We will rejoice and be glad in it.

Alleluia!

Ingram Content Group UK Ltd.
Milton Keynes UK
UKHW021302250623
424008UK00021B/490